260 Things to Know About Franchising a Fast Food Chain

Disclaimer:

The information contained in this book is provided for general informational purposes only. While every effort has been made to ensure the accuracy and completeness of the information contained herein, the author and publisher make no guarantees, either express or implied, about the suitability, reliability, availability, timeliness, or accuracy of the information contained within.

The author and publisher of this book do not assume any legal or other liability or responsibility whatsoever for any errors, omissions, or inaccuracies, nor for any consequences that may arise from the use of the information contained herein. Furthermore, the inclusion of any terms or definitions in this book does not imply endorsement or recommendation of any particular concept, product, or service.

It is the responsibility of the reader to independently verify the accuracy and applicability of any information contained in this book. The reader is advised to seek professional advice before making any decisions based on the information contained herein. The author and publisher disclaim any and all liability for any loss or damage arising from reliance on the information contained in this book.

Table of Contents

Introduction

Franchising a fast food chain has become a popular way of expanding business in recent years. It offers the opportunity for entrepreneurs to run their own business under an established brand name and with the support of a franchisor. However, before investing in a franchise, there are several things to consider and understand about the process.

This book aims to provide a comprehensive glossary of terms and definitions related to franchising a fast food chain. It covers everything from the different types of franchise agreements to the franchise disclosure document, and from franchisor support to franchise fees. The definitions are presented in an easy-to-understand format, making it a valuable resource for anyone looking to enter the world of franchising. Whether you are a prospective franchisee or a franchisor, this book will assist you in navigating the complex world of fast food chain franchising.

Ad Fund Committee

A committee composed of franchisor and franchisee representatives responsible for managing the advertising fund and deciding how it will be spent.

Advertising Fund

A portion of franchise fees and royalties that are collected by the franchisor and pooled together for advertising and marketing purposes to benefit the entire franchise network.

Agreement

A legal contract between the franchisor and franchisee that outlines the terms and conditions of the business relationship, including fees, royalties, and operational guidelines.

Agreement Renewal

The process through which a franchise agreement is extended for a certain period, subject to the terms of the agreement.

Agreement Termination

The cancellation of a franchise agreement before its agreed-upon expiration date, typically due to a breach of the agreement's terms.

Annual Franchise Fee

The annual fee that a franchisee pays to a franchisor for the right to use their brand name, products, and services.

Area Developer

A franchisee who is granted the right to develop and manage multiple locations within a specific geographic area.

Area Development Agreement

A legal agreement between a franchisor and a franchisee outlining the obligations of both parties for multiple franchise units in a specific geographic area.

Area Representative

A person or entity designated by a franchisor to act as an intermediary between the franchisor and franchisees in a specific geographic area.

Asset Purchase Agreement

A contract outlining the terms and conditions of the sale of a franchisee's existing franchise unit to a third party.

Assistance with Site Selection

The support provided by a franchisor to a franchisee in selecting a suitable location for their franchise unit.

Assistance with Store Design and Layout

The support provided by a franchisor to a franchisee in designing and laying out their franchise unit's physical space.

Audit

A process of reviewing a franchised location's financial statements, records, and operations to ensure compliance with the franchisor's standards and requirements.

Authorized Territory

The geographic area within which a franchisee is allowed to operate their franchise.

Awarding a Franchise

The process through which a franchisor selects and approves a franchisee to operate a new franchise unit.

Balance Sheet

A financial statement that provides an overview of a fast food franchise's assets, liabilities, and equity at a given point in time. This document provides insight into the financial health of the franchise and is used to track progress and identify areas for improvement.

Banking Relationship

The relationship between a fast food franchise and its bank or other financial institutions. This partnership helps provide access to capital for growth and development, as well as important financial services such as credit card processing and payroll.

Bookkeeping

The process of recording and reconciling financial transactions for a fast food franchise. This includes everything from sales and expenses to payroll and tax filings. Accurate bookkeeping is critical for maintaining financial stability and complying with legal requirements.

Brand

A term used to describe the name, logo, and visual elements associated with a fast food chain. A strong brand is important in franchising to help attract customers and promote consistency across all locations. It also helps with marketing and advertising efforts.

Brand Standards

A set of guidelines that dictate how a fast food franchise should look, feel, and operate. Brand standards ensure consistency across all locations and help maintain the integrity of the brand.

Break-even Point

The point at which a fast food franchise generates enough revenue to cover all of its expenses. This is an important milestone for any business and is calculated by dividing the total fixed costs by the gross profit margin.

Build-out

The process of constructing and outfitting a fast food franchise location. This includes everything from designing the layout, installing equipment, and decorating the space. Build-out costs can vary widely depending on factors such as location, size, and the specific needs of the franchise.

Business Advisor

A professional who provides guidance and advice to fast food franchise owners on a variety of topics, including financial planning, marketing, and operations. Working with a business advisor can help improve the success and profitability of a franchise.

Business Entity

The legal structure used to operate a fast food franchise. This may include a sole proprietorship, partnership, corporation, or limited liability company (LLC). Choosing the right business entity is important for ensuring proper tax treatment and liability protection.

Business Insurance

Insurance policies designed to protect a fast food franchise from various types of risks, including liability, property damage, and employee injuries. This is an important investment for any business to minimize financial losses and protect against lawsuits.

Business License

A legal document required to operate a fast food franchise in a particular jurisdiction. This may include permits for food service, zoning, advertising, and other activities.

Business License Compliance

The process of ensuring that a fast food franchise complies with all legal requirements for operating in a specific jurisdiction. This includes obtaining the proper licenses and permits, maintaining proper business records, and complying with health and safety regulations. Failure to comply can result in fines, legal action, and reputational damage.

Business Model

The method and approach used by a fast food chain to generate revenue and profits. In franchising, the business model is typically replicated across all locations to maintain consistency and brand integrity. It includes everything from menu offerings, pricing, staffing, and marketing strategies.

Business Operations

The day-to-day activities involved in running a fast food franchise, including ordering supplies, managing employees, handling customer complaints, and financial reporting. Effective operations are crucial for maintaining consistency and quality across all franchise locations.

Business Plan

A written document that outlines the details of a fast food franchise, including goals, objectives, financial projections, and marketing strategies. A business plan is critical for obtaining financing and establishing a roadmap for future growth and development.

Capital

The financial resources required to start and operate a fast food franchise. Capital includes the franchise fee, initial investment costs, and ongoing expenses associated with running the business, such as staff salaries, equipment, and inventory.

Competition

Other fast food chains competing for customers within the same market. Franchisees need to stay aware of their competitors' strategies to stand out with unique offerings, excellent customer service, and efficient operations.

Compliance

The adherence to the standards established by the franchisor and any applicable laws and regulations. Compliance is essential to maintaining the integrity of the brand and avoiding legal penalties.

Concept

The unique business model of a fast food chain that includes menu offerings, branding, and operational processes. Concept development is crucial to franchise growth and success. A franchisee needs to adhere to the concept guidelines established by the franchisor to guarantee that customers receive a consistent experience across all locations.

Confidential Operations Manual

The guide provided by the franchisor that contains detailed information about the operation of the franchise. The confidential operations manual outlines the policies and procedures that franchisees must follow and plays a critical role in maintaining consistency across all locations.

Consumer Trends

The changing preferences and behavior of customers. Keeping up to date with consumer trends is vital for franchisees to remain competitive and ensure that their menu offerings are aligned with customer demand.

Continuous Improvement

The approach franchisees take to improve their operations consistently. Continuous improvement includes refining the menu, enhancing customer service, and optimizing operations for maximum efficiency.

Contract

A legally binding agreement between the franchisor and franchisee that outlines the rights and obligations of both parties. The franchise contract includes the terms of use for the franchisor's intellectual property, the franchise fee, and the franchisee's responsibilities related to the operation of the franchise.

Control

The amount of power the franchisor has over the franchisee's business operations. Franchisees follow strict guidelines set by the franchisor, limiting their control over day-to-day operations. However, the franchisor provides robust support that can help the franchisee maintain consistency and achieve success.

Convenience

The ease of use for the customer, including location, hours of operation, ordering options, and payment methods. Providing convenience is critical to attracting and retaining customers, especially in the fast food industry, where customers seek quick and hassle-free experiences.

Conversion

The process of changing an existing restaurant into a fast food franchise. Conversion involves rebranding, redesigning the restaurant layout, and implementing the franchisor's operating systems, menus, and marketing strategies.

Cooperative Advertising

Advertising initiatives managed by the franchisor, in which franchisees contribute funds. Cooperative advertising is designed to drive business to all franchise locations, and it is a cost-effective way for franchisees to benefit from advertising that typically would be too expensive for them to undertake independently.

Corporate Support

Assistance provided by the franchisor to the franchisee in various areas, including site selection, training, advertising, and operational support. Corporate support is essential to help franchisees achieve success and maintain the standards set by the franchisor.

Cross-training

The practice of training employees across multiple departments or roles. Cross-training provides employees with diverse skill sets, increases productivity, and promotes employee engagement and retention.

Customer Experience

The impression a customer gains from the interaction with the franchise, including service quality, speed, and convenience. Creating a positive customer experience is paramount to the success of any fast food franchise because it drives repeat business and customer loyalty.

Default

A violation of the terms of the franchise agreement by the franchisee. This can include failure to pay royalties or other fees, failure to maintain required standards of operation, or other breaches of contract.

Demographics

The characteristics of a specific group of people, often categorized by age, gender, income level, and other factors. Demographic data is important for franchises in order to target their marketing efforts and tailor their products and services to the needs and preferences of their customers.

Development Agreement

A legal document that outlines the rights and responsibilities of both the franchisor and franchisee regarding the development of a specific number of franchised units within a given territory. The agreement typically includes details such as deadlines, financial obligations, and performance expectations.

Development Fee

A fee paid by the franchisee to the franchisor in order to secure the right to develop additional franchise locations within a specific territory. This fee can be significant and is typically non-refundable, even if the development does not proceed as planned.

Development Schedule

A timeline outlining the expected milestones and deadlines for the development of new franchise locations within a given territory. This can include benchmarks such as site selection, construction, and grand opening.

Digital Marketing

A broad term that encompasses various online marketing techniques, such as social media marketing, search engine optimization (SEO), and pay-per-click (PPC) advertising. It is an important component of modern marketing strategies and can help franchises reach a wider audience.

Direct Mail Advertising

A marketing strategy that involves sending promotional materials, such as coupons and flyers, directly to potential customers through the mail. This method can be effective in generating new business and increasing brand awareness.

Disclosure Document

A document that the franchisor must provide to potential franchisees before they sign a franchise agreement. It contains important information about the franchisor and the franchise system, including the history of the business, the initial and ongoing costs of the franchise, and the terms and conditions of the agreement.

Disclosure Requirements

The legal requirements for franchisors to disclose certain information to potential franchisees. This information typically includes the franchisor's financial statements, the identity and business experience of key executives, and certain details regarding the franchise system and the terms of the franchise agreement.

Dispute Resolution

The process by which the franchisor and franchisee attempt to resolve disagreements or conflicts that may arise during the course of their business relationship. This can include mediation, arbitration, or litigation.

Distribution System

The system used by the franchisor to distribute products or services to franchisees. This can include various methods such as direct shipment, centralized warehousing, or a combination of the two.

down Payment

The initial payment made by the franchisee when signing a franchise agreement. This payment typically represents a portion of the total initial investment and is typically non-refundable.

Dress Code

The guidelines and rules regarding the appearance of employees in a franchise location. Uniforms or other dress code requirements may be mandated in order to maintain a consistent brand image and ensure a professional appearance.

Dual Distribution

A strategy in which a franchisor simultaneously sells products or services directly to consumers while also franchising the same products or services to independent franchisees. This strategy can have both advantages and disadvantages for the franchisor and franchisees.

Due Diligence

The process of researching and evaluating a potential investment, such as a franchise opportunity. It involves gathering relevant information and assessing the risks and benefits of the investment before making a decision.

Establishment Costs

The costs associated with setting up and launching a franchise including equipment, licenses, marketing, and training costs.

Fast Casual

A restaurant concept that falls somewhere between fast food and casual dining, offering higher quality ingredients and a more upscale atmosphere than traditional fast food chains. Fast casual restaurants are typically priced higher than fast food, but lower than casual dining, and often offer customizable menus and online ordering options.

Fixed Costs

Business expenses that do not vary based on sales volume, such as rent, salaries, and utilities. Fixed costs are an important consideration for franchisees, as they can have a significant impact on profitability and cash flow.

Food Safety

The measures taken to ensure the quality and safety of the food served at a fast food chain, including proper preparation, storage, and handling techniques. Food safety is a critical concern for franchisees, as violations can result in fines, legal action, and damage to the brand's reputation.

Franchise Agreement

A legally binding contract between the franchisor and franchisee that outlines the terms and conditions of the franchise relationship, including the rights and obligations of both parties. The agreement typically covers areas such as the initial fee, ongoing royalties, intellectual property rights, training and support, and termination provisions.

Franchise Disclosure Document (FDD)

A legal document required by the Federal Trade Commission that provides potential franchisees with detailed information about the franchisor, including financial statements, fees, and obligations. The FDD also outlines the terms of the franchise agreement, such as territory restrictions, non-compete clauses, and termination rights.

Franchise Fee

The upfront cost paid by the franchisee to the franchisor for the right to operate a fast food chain under their brand. The franchise fee typically covers the initial training and support provided by the franchisor, as well as access to their proprietary systems and technology.

Franchise Marketing

The marketing initiatives and support provided by the franchisor to promote the fast food chain and drive customer traffic to franchise locations. Franchise marketing may include national advertising campaigns, local store marketing programs, and online promotions.

Franchise Renewal

The process by which a franchisee extends their franchise agreement with the franchisor beyond its initial term. Renewal typically involves a review of the franchisee's performance and compliance with the terms of the franchise agreement.

Franchise Royalties

The ongoing fees paid by the franchisee to the franchisor for the right to operate a fast food chain under their brand. Royalties are typically calculated as a percentage of the franchisee's gross revenue and cover ongoing support, marketing, research and development, and other expenses.

Franchise Support

The ongoing training, marketing, and operational assistance provided by the franchisor to franchisees. Franchise support is designed to help franchisees maximize their profitability and maintain consistent quality and standards across all franchise locations.

Franchise Territory

The geographic area in which the franchisee has the exclusive right to operate a fast food chain under the franchisor's brand. Territory restrictions are an important consideration for franchisees, as they can impact the potential for growth and profitability of the business.

Franchise Training

The initial and ongoing training provided by the franchisor to franchisees and their employees on operating procedures, product preparation, customer service, and other aspects of the business. Franchise training is often a key factor in the success of franchisees, as it helps ensure consistency and quality across all locations.

Franchisee

A person or group that purchases the right to operate a fast food chain in a specific location, typically in exchange for a franchise fee and ongoing royalties paid to the franchisor. Franchisees are responsible for managing the day-to-day operations of their franchise location, including hiring and training employees, maintaining equipment, and marketing the business within their local community.

Franchisee Association

An organization formed by franchisees to represent their interests and advocate for their rights within the franchising system. Franchisee associations may provide resources, support, and networking opportunities for franchisees, as well as a forum for addressing common concerns with the franchisor.

Franchisor

The entity that owns the overall rights and trademarks to a fast food chain and provides the franchisee with access to their brand, operating systems, and marketing materials. The franchisor is responsible for setting the standards and guidelines for franchisees to operate their businesses, including training programs, ongoing support, and marketing initiatives.

Generic Products

Fast food franchises may sell generic products, such as cups, napkins, and uniforms, to their franchisees. These products typically feature the franchiser's logo or other branding, and the franchiser may require franchisees to purchase them from specific suppliers.

Geographic Territory

A specific area or region in which a fast food franchisee is granted exclusive rights to operate their business is known as a geographic territory. A franchisee may be responsible for multiple territories, and the size of each territory can vary depending on the franchiser's rules and agreements.

Goals

Franchisees should have specific goals that they aim to achieve within a certain timeframe, such as increasing revenue by a certain percentage or opening a certain number of new locations. Setting clear, measurable goals is important for keeping a franchisee focused and motivated.

Goodwill

The value of a fast food chain's brand recognition, reputation, and customer loyalty is often referred to as goodwill. Goodwill can be an important factor in a franchisee's success and profitability, as it can draw customers to the franchise's location.

Grand Opening

The inaugural launch event or celebration for a new fast food franchise location, usually marked by special promotions, discounts, and giveaways. A successful grand opening event can generate excitement and draw in customers.

Grievance Procedure

Franchisees typically have a process for airing grievances or disagreements with the franchiser, known as a grievance procedure. This may involve submitting a written complaint, attending a mediation or arbitration session, or following a set of established rules or protocols.

Gross Margin

The difference between a fast food franchise's revenue and the cost of goods sold is known as the gross margin. A high gross margin indicates that the franchise is operating efficiently and earning more profit.

Gross Sales

The amount of revenue generated by a fast food franchise, including all sales made through each location, is known as gross sales. Gross sales are important for determining the franchisee's profits and for meeting contractual obligations to the franchiser, such as paying royalties.

Group Purchasing

Franchisees may be able to take advantage of group purchasing power by buying supplies, equipment, and other products together as part of a larger franchise network. This can result in lower prices and more bargaining power.

Growth Strategies

Different methods and procedures used to increase the size
and success of a fast food chain are referred to as growth
strategies. These may include expanding the number of
locations, introducing new menu items, implementing
marketing campaigns, and maximizing revenue from
existing locations.

Guaranteed Minimum Sales

Some franchisers offer a guaranteed minimum level of sales
to their franchisees as a way of reducing risk and increasing
confidence. This means that the franchiser will provide
financial compensation to the franchisee if their sales do not
meet a certain threshold.

Guest Experience

The overall experience that customers have when visiting a
fast food franchise is referred to as the guest experience.
Good guest experiences can lead to increased customer
loyalty and positive reviews, while poor experiences can
harm a franchisee's reputation and revenue.

Guest Feedback

Collecting and analyzing customer feedback is an important part of operating a successful fast food franchise. Franchisees may use various methods to solicit feedback, such as customer surveys, social media monitoring, and comment cards.

Guest Loyalty Programs

Some fast food franchises offer loyalty programs that reward customers for repeat business or for referring friends and family. These programs can help to increase customer retention and attract new business.

Initial Training

A comprehensive program provided by the franchisor to teach the franchisee or their managers how to operate the fast food chain's business model. The franchisor may require an on-site training program or online modules to ensure consistency in management and customer service.

Insurance

A form of risk management that protects the franchisor and franchisee from financial losses resulting from accidents, natural disasters or other unforeseen events that result in property damage, injuries, or litigation.

Intellectual Property

The trademarks, logos, and trade secrets that define a fast food chain's brand identity. Franchisors carefully guard their intellectual property (IP) by requiring franchisees to adhere to strict branding guidelines and operating procedures.

Inventory Control

A system that ensures the right amount of inventory is in stock to meet customer demand without overstocking and causing waste. Franchisees must adhere to strict inventory control procedures to maintain profitability and reduce waste.

Investment

The amount of money required to start a franchised fast food chain, which includes fees, equipment, inventory and any real estate purchases or leases. The potential ROI (return on investment) is a crucial factor in determining whether franchising is a worthwhile endeavor.

Jake Food

Jake Food is a fast food chain franchise that offers all-in-one meals in liquid form, providing customers with a balanced and convenient meal option that can be consumed on-the-go. The Jake Food franchise model targets health-conscious consumers with busy lifestyles who value nutrition and efficiency. The franchise offers support in areas such as location selection, equipment, operations, marketing, and logistics. Jake Food franchises can be owned by individuals or groups, with investment costs and revenue potential varying depending on location and market demand.

Jib Management

JIB Management is a fast food chain franchise that focuses on Mexican-style food, such as tacos, burritos, and nachos. The franchise model offers flexible ownership options, such as single-unit, multi-unit, area development, or master franchise agreements. The franchisor provides support in areas such as operational training, real estate and site selection, marketing, and supply chain management. Franchisees must comply with brand standards and guidelines and participate in ongoing training and quality assurance programs. JIB Management aims to expand its franchise network through strategic partnerships and innovation in menu and service offerings.

Job Description

A job description in franchising outlines the duties and responsibilities of a position within the fast food chain, whether it is a corporate or franchisee-owned location. Clear job descriptions can help attract qualified candidates, establish performance expectations, and facilitate communication between the franchisor and franchisee. It should include information such as job title, summary of key tasks and objectives, qualifications and prerequisites, reporting structure, and performance metrics. The job description should be periodically reviewed and updated to ensure alignment with the franchise's growth and operational strategies.

Joint Agreement

A joint agreement in franchising is a contractual arrangement between two or more parties that outlines their roles, responsibilities, and obligations in operating a fast food chain. Joint agreements can take various forms, such as joint ventures, joint promotions, joint marketing agreements, joint licenses, or joint ownership models. Joint agreements help reduce risk, increase revenue potential, and leverage the strengths of the parties involved, but also require clear communication, trust, and alignment of goals and values.

Joint Check

Joint check in franchising is a payment method that allows a franchisee to issue a check to a supplier jointly with the franchisor. This method helps ensure that the supplier is paid on time and that the franchisee is using the correct vendor designated by the franchisor. Joint checks may also allow for cost savings through bulk purchasing and negotiations. However, it is important to ensure that the use of joint checks is clearly defined in the franchise agreement and that all parties are aware of their roles and responsibilities.

Joint Development Agreement

A joint development agreement in franchising is a legal contract between a franchisor and one or more partner companies to jointly develop and launch a new fast food chain concept. The agreement typically outlines the responsibilities and contributions of each party, intellectual property rights, financial arrangements, and project milestones. Joint development agreements can benefit both the franchisor and partner companies by leveraging each other's expertise, resources, and market reach. However, it requires a high level of collaboration and trust among all parties involved and carries significant legal and financial risks.

Joint License

A joint license in franchising is a legal agreement between two or more entities to share intellectual property or technology rights for a fast food chain concept. Joint licenses are common in the fast food industry, where franchise businesses often rely on proprietary recipes, systems, equipment, or branding. Joint licenses can provide cost savings, increased revenue, and innovation opportunities, but require clear definitions of intellectual property rights, revenue sharing arrangements, and dispute resolution mechanisms.

Joint Marketing

Joint marketing in franchising is a cooperative effort between franchisors and franchisees or between different franchises to promote a common brand or product. Joint marketing activities can include social media campaigns, loyalty programs, print and digital advertising, PR, or special events. Joint marketing can provide cost savings, increased brand awareness, and cross-selling opportunities. Clear agreements and guidelines should be established to ensure fairness, alignment, and compliance with brand standards and legal requirements.

Joint Ownership

Joint ownership in franchising refers to a partnership or co-ownership arrangement between two or more parties in operating a fast food chain. Joint ownership may apply to franchise businesses, where franchisors and franchisees share ownership of intellectual property, operational systems, or financial outcomes. Joint ownership can provide cost savings, increased revenue potential, and leverage the strengths of each party, but also requires clear definitions of roles and responsibilities, legal and financial agreements, and conflict resolution mechanisms.

Joint Promotion

Joint promotion in franchising is a marketing strategy that involves multiple franchisors or franchisees collaborating to promote a common brand, product, or service. Joint promotions can provide cost savings, increased exposure, and cross-selling opportunities, but require careful planning and communication to avoid conflicts and ensure fairness. Joint promotions may include customer loyalty programs, promotional events, cross-promotional discounts, or co-branded advertising campaigns. Joint promotions can be an effective way to leverage the strength of the franchise network while also fostering collaboration and community building among franchisees.

Joint Venture

A joint venture in franchising is an agreement between two or more parties to contribute capital and expertise to establish and operate a new fast food chain. The parties involved in a joint venture may be individuals or companies with complementary strengths that make a successful partnership. Joint ventures allow for sharing of resources, risk, and profits, but also require clear communication, trust, and a solid understanding of legal and financial obligations.

Jollibee

Jollibee is a Filipino fast food chain franchise that features a mix of Filipino, American, and Asian cuisine, such as fried chicken, spaghetti, and peach-mango pies. The Jollibee franchise model emphasizes its unique brand identity, family-oriented culture, and customer service excellence. The franchisor provides support in areas such as site selection and development, training, marketing, and supply chain management. Franchisees must comply with brand standards and quality assurance measures, but also have some flexibility to adapt to local tastes and preferences. Jollibee aims to expand its global presence through partnerships and acquisition of local fast food chains.

Jurisdiction

Jurisdiction in franchising refers to the legal authority of a governing body, such as a state or a country, to regulate and oversee franchising activities. Franchise businesses are subject to various laws and regulations that vary by jurisdiction, such as disclosure requirements, registration fees, and operational standards. It is important for franchisors and franchisees to understand the scope and limitations of jurisdiction in the countries or states where they operate, to avoid legal and financial risks.

Just Falafel

Just Falafel is a fast food chain franchise that specializes in Middle Eastern cuisine, such as falafel, hummus, and shawarma. The franchise model targets a diverse and health-conscious customer base, emphasizing fresh and flavorful vegetarian and vegan options. The Just Falafel franchise offers support in areas such as site selection, design, training, marketing, and IT systems. Franchisees must comply with brand standards and quality assurance measures, as well as local regulations and customs. Just Falafel aims to expand its franchise network globally through strategic partnerships and innovation in menu and service offerings.

Just Salad

Just Salad is a fast food chain franchise that focuses on healthy and sustainable food options, including salads, wraps, bowls, and soups. The franchise model emphasizes its commitment to ethical and eco-friendly practices, such as using locally-sourced ingredients, biodegradable packaging, and energy-efficient operations. The Just Salad franchise offers support in areas such as site selection, training, marketing, and technology. Franchisees must share the values and mission of the brand and comply with operational and marketing standards set by the franchisor.

Key Performance Indicators (KPIs)

Metrics used to measure the success of a franchise, such as sales revenue, customer retention, and employee productivity. KPIs allow franchise owners and managers to track performance over time and make data-driven decisions about how to improve operations. KPIs can be customized based on the specific needs of each franchise and should be regularly reviewed to ensure the franchise is meeting its goals.

Kick-off Meeting

A meeting between the franchisor and franchisee to set expectations, review franchise documents, and establish goals and timelines for opening the franchise. The kick-off meeting provides an opportunity for both parties to discuss any concerns or questions before moving forward with the franchising process. It is an essential part of the franchisee's due diligence and should include key stakeholders from both the franchisor and franchisee's teams.

Kiosk

A self-contained, standalone structure that is typically smaller than a traditional restaurant and designed to serve a limited menu of popular items quickly and efficiently. Kiosks are often located in high-traffic areas like malls, airports, or train stations, and are ideal for franchises looking to expand their reach to new markets without investing in a full-scale restaurant. They can also be a more cost-effective way to operate a franchise, as they require less space and personnel than a traditional restaurant.

Kiosk Franchise

A franchise model that operates through self-contained structures located in high-traffic areas. Kiosk franchises are often smaller than traditional restaurants and are designed to serve a limited menu quickly and efficiently. This franchise model is ideal for entrepreneurs looking to start a franchise with minimal investment, as it requires less space and personnel than a traditional restaurant. Kiosk franchises can offer a range of food options, including snacks, drinks, and fast food.

Kiosk Location

The physical location of a kiosk franchise, which can have a significant impact on its success. Franchisees should research and select a location that has high foot traffic and is easily accessible to customers. Factors to consider when choosing a kiosk location include proximity to other businesses, nearby events, and local demographics. Many franchisors offer support and guidance to franchisees in selecting kiosk locations, including market research, site visits, and lease negotiations.

Kiosk Operations

The day-to-day activities required to run a kiosk franchise, including inventory management, cash handling, and customer service. Kiosk operations are essential to the success of a fast food franchise and require careful planning and execution. Franchisees should develop standard operating procedures for all kiosk operations and train employees on these procedures regularly. Kiosk operations should be regularly reviewed and updated to ensure maximum efficiency and profitability. Franchisees can also utilize management software and other digital tools to streamline kiosk operations and improve overall franchise performance.

Kiosk Technology

The digital tools and devices used to automate and streamline operations in a kiosk franchise. Kiosk technology can include point-of-sale (POS) systems, self-ordering kiosks, digital menu boards, and mobile ordering apps. These tools can reduce wait times, improve order accuracy, and increase customer satisfaction. Franchisees should choose kiosk technology that is user-friendly, reliable, and integrates with other systems in the franchise.

Kiosk Vendor

A supplier of kiosks and related equipment for franchises. Kiosk vendors offer a range of products and services, including kiosk design and installation, equipment leasing, and ongoing support and maintenance. Choosing the right kiosk vendor is an essential part of launching a kiosk franchise and requires careful research and due diligence. Factors to consider when choosing a kiosk vendor include cost, quality of equipment, customer support, and industry reputation.

Kitchen Equipment

All the necessary equipment needed to operate a fast food chain, including ovens, fryers, grills, and refrigerators. Kitchen equipment is an essential investment for any fast food franchise, as it impacts food quality, productivity, and employee safety. Franchise owners should research and invest in high-quality, durable equipment and ensure that it meets all necessary health and safety regulations.

Kitchen Layouts

The physical arrangement of equipment, workstations, and appliances in a fast food restaurant's kitchen. An efficient layout can improve workflow, reduce wait times, and maximize productivity. There are different types of kitchen layouts, such as the assembly line layout, which moves food through a linear process from preparation to service, and the zone layout, which organizes the kitchen into different functional areas for specific tasks. Choosing the right layout depends on the franchise's menu, size, and operational needs.

Kitchen Safety

The set of practices and procedures that ensure employees and customers are safe in a fast food restaurant's kitchen. Kitchen safety includes equipment maintenance, proper handling of food and chemicals, fire safety protocols, and employee training on safety best practices. Franchisees are responsible for complying with all health and safety regulations and providing a safe working environment for their employees. Kitchen safety should be a top priority for franchise owners and managers, as it impacts employee morale, customer trust, and franchise reputation.

Know-how

The knowledge, skills and expertise required to successfully operate a fast food franchise. This includes understanding the brand's values, menu, operations, and customer service expectations. Franchisees should receive comprehensive training from the franchisor to gain the necessary know-how to run a successful business. This could include on-site training, virtual training, and ongoing support from the franchise network.

Knowledge Management

The process of capturing, distributing, and utilizing knowledge within a fast food franchise. Knowledge management ensures that franchise employees have access to current and accurate information, such as operating procedures, product knowledge, and customer service training. Knowledge management can improve franchise performance by reducing errors, increasing productivity, and supporting innovation. Franchisees can implement knowledge management systems through online training programs, franchise manuals, and virtual collaboration tools.

Kpi Benchmarking

The process of comparing a fast food franchise's key performance indicators (KPIs) to industry standards and best practices. Benchmarking can help franchisees identify areas where they need to improve and set realistic goals for growth. Common KPIs used in benchmarking include sales growth, customer satisfaction, employee turnover, and profit margins. Franchisees can use benchmarking data to improve operational efficiency, enhance customer experience, and increase profitability.

Kpi Dashboard

A real-time dashboard that displays key performance indicators (KPIs) for a fast food franchise. The dashboard shows franchise owners and managers how the business is performing and allows them to make data-driven decisions. Many franchisors offer KPI dashboards as part of their franchise management systems, which can include features like data visualization, custom reporting, and alerts for performance issues.

Labor Costs

The expenses associated with hiring and paying employees to work in the fast food franchise. This can include salaries, wages, and benefits such as healthcare and retirement plans.

Launch Costs

The initial expenses associated with opening a fast food franchise, including equipment, inventory, marketing, and other start-up costs.

Lease Agreement

A contract that outlines the terms and conditions of renting or leasing space for a fast food franchise. This includes the duration of the lease, rent payments, and any restrictions or requirements for the property.

Legal Compliance

The requirement for the fast food franchise to abide by all federal, state, and local laws and regulations related to operating a restaurant. This includes food safety regulations, labor laws, and tax regulations.

Liability Insurance

Protection against legal claims and lawsuits that may result from accidents or injuries that occur in or around the fast food franchise. This type of insurance can cover legal fees, medical expenses, and damages awarded in court.

Licensing

A legal agreement between the franchisor and franchisee that allows the franchisee to use the franchisor's logo, name, and operating procedures in exchange for a fee. Unlike franchising, licensing does not provide ongoing support and training from the franchisor.

Liquidated Damages

Pre-determined penalties for a franchisee's failure to meet certain obligations outlined in the franchise agreement. These may include penalties for failing to maintain the franchise's standards, breaches of confidentiality, or other violations of the agreement.

Loan

A financial agreement in which the franchisee borrows money from a lender to cover start-up costs or other expenses related to the fast food franchise. Loans may come with interest rates, repayment schedules, and other terms and conditions.

Local Marketing

Promotional activities that target the local community and increase awareness of the fast food franchise. This can include advertising in local media, participating in community events, and sponsoring local sports teams.

Local Regulations

Regulations specific to the region or municipality where the fast food franchise is located. This can include zoning regulations, building codes, and other laws that may impact the franchise's operations.

Location

The physical address where the fast food franchise will be located. Choosing the right location is critical for success, as it can impact foot traffic, accessibility, and competition with other nearby businesses.

Logo

The visual representation of the fast food franchise, which is used for marketing and branding purposes. This may include a combination of words, graphics, and colors that create a recognizable image.

Long-term Contracts

Agreements that extend beyond the initial franchise term and provide the franchisee with additional rights and benefits. These may include the right to renew the franchise agreement or purchase additional franchises at a reduced rate.

Losses

Financial losses that may be incurred when operating a fast food franchise. These can include unexpected expenses, slow sales periods, and other factors that negatively impact the franchise's profitability.

Loyalty Programs

Incentive programs designed to encourage repeat business from customers. These can include offering discounts or rewards for frequent visits or purchases.

Management Training

This is the training program provided by the franchisor to assist franchisees with the day-to-day management of the fast food restaurant. This includes training on handling finances, employee management, marketing, and other essential business operations.

Mandatory Software

Software that must be used by franchisees to manage the day-to-day operations of the restaurant. This may include inventory management, ordering and payments processing.

Market Research

This is the process of gathering essential information used to identify the viability of a fast food franchise in a particular area. It helps to identify potential customers, location, competition, and the feasibility of the fast food chain.

Marketing Fee

This is a fee that franchisees are required to pay to the franchisor for marketing and advertising efforts. This fee is used to fund marketing campaigns and promote the brand.

Marketing Fund

This is a fund in which franchisees are required to contribute to for advertising and promoting the entire franchise network. The purpose of this fund is to ensure the success of the overall franchise and to increase brand awareness.

Marketing Plan

This is a plan developed by the franchisor that outlines the strategies and tactics to be used to promote the brand and attract customers. The marketing plan is typically a comprehensive plan that includes details about advertising, public relations, social media, and other marketing efforts.

Marketing Support

The support provided by the franchisor to help franchisees with marketing and advertising efforts. This can include marketing materials, advertising campaigns, and assistance with local marketing initiatives.

Master Franchise

This is a type of franchise agreement in which the franchisee secures the right to develop and sub-franchise a specific geographic area.

Master License Agreement

This type of agreement grants the rights to sub-franchise a specific geographic territory to a franchisee. The franchisee must then manage and develop the franchise in the assigned territory.

Menu Engineering

This is the process of evaluating the menu items offered by the fast food chain, to determine which items are most profitable and which items should be eliminated. This helps the franchise owner to understand the profit margin of each menu item and make decisions about what to offer customers.

Menu Testing

This is the process of testing new menu items to ensure that they are popular and profitable before they are added to the menu. This helps to minimize waste and ensure that the new menu item will be successful once it is introduced to customers.

Minor Refurbishments

Minor repairs or renovation work done in the restaurant, such as a refresh of the decor, minor maintenance or repairs to equipment.

Monthly Royalties

The percentage of revenue that a franchisee must pay to the franchisor every month. This is typically a fixed percentage of the franchisee's monthly revenue and is outlined in the franchise agreement.

Multi-brand Strategy

A business strategy that involves owning and operating several different fast food franchise brands. This can help to increase revenue and diversify the franchisee's portfolio.

Multi-unit Franchisee

A franchisee that owns and operates more than one franchise location. This type of franchisee is responsible for managing multiple locations and must have extensive management skills and experience.

National Advertising Fund

A fund created by a franchise brand where a certain percentage of fees paid by franchisees is allocated for advertising on a national level. The National Advertising Fund helps promote the franchise brand as a whole and typically covers advertising expenses such as TV commercials, online ads, and print media. This is beneficial for franchisees as they do not need to worry about the cost and implementation of promoting the brand on a national level, leaving them to focus on the local marketing efforts for their own location.

Net Worth

This is the total value of assets (property, investments, cash, etc.) minus the total amount of liabilities (debts, loans, etc.). When considering franchising a fast food chain, the franchisor may require a certain minimum net worth before allowing a franchisee to operate a franchise. The reason for this is because the franchisor wants to ensure that the franchisee has sufficient financial stability to run the franchise successfully. This requirement varies from brand to brand and can range from tens of thousands to millions of dollars, depending on the size and popularity of the brand.

Non-compete Agreement

A legal contract that prohibits a franchisee from starting a competing business at the termination of the franchise agreement. The purpose of this agreement is to protect the franchisor's intellectual property, trade secrets and other confidential information, as well as to prevent the franchisee from benefiting from the training and support from the franchise system, then using that knowledge to compete against them. The non-compete period may last for a certain number of years or indefinitely, and violating the agreement may result in legal action being taken against the franchisee.

Non-refundable Fees

These are fees paid by the franchisee to the franchisor that are not refundable, such as the initial franchise fee or ongoing royalties. Non-refundable fees are used to cover the costs of training, ongoing support, marketing, and other expenses associated with operating the franchise system. It is important for potential franchisees to understand the amount of non-refundable fees associated with a franchise system before signing the franchise agreement, as it is a significant investment that cannot be recouped if the franchisee later decides to terminate the agreement.

Onboarding

The process of training new employees and bringing them up to speed on the restaurant's policies and procedures. This is important for ensuring that all employees are able to provide consistent service to customers.

Ongoing Support

Assistance provided by the franchisor to the franchisee after the restaurant is up and running. It includes marketing support, ongoing training, and periodic reviews to ensure compliance with the franchisor's standards.

Online Ordering

A service offered by some fast-food chains that allows customers to place orders online for delivery or pickup. This has become increasingly popular in recent years as more people use smartphones and other devices to order food.

Opening Assistance

Services provided by the franchisor to help the franchisee set up the new restaurant. It includes site selection, lease negotiation, and a comprehensive training program.

Opening Inventory

The initial inventory of food and supplies that is ordered by the franchisee in preparation for the restaurant's opening.

Operating Costs

The expenses associated with running the restaurant, including rent, utilities, food and supply costs, employee salaries and benefits, and marketing expenses.

Operational Efficiency

The ability of a fast-food chain to efficiently produce and deliver food to customers. This includes minimizing waste, reducing wait times, and increasing the speed of service.

Operations Audit

An evaluation conducted by a franchisor to ensure that the franchisee is operating the restaurant in compliance with the franchisor's standards. This can include everything from food quality to employee training.

Operations Manager

A person employed by the franchisee to oversee the day-to-day operations of the restaurant. He or she is responsible for ensuring that the restaurant is running smoothly and that all policies and procedures are being followed.

Operations Manual

A detailed guide that provides step-by-step procedures for running the restaurant. It includes everything from how to prepare the food to how to handle customer complaints.

Order Accuracy

The degree to which a fast-food chain is able to accurately fulfill customer orders. This is important for customer satisfaction and can impact the restaurant's bottom line.

Order Fulfillment

The process of receiving and processing customer orders.
This includes taking the order, preparing the food, and
delivering it to the customer or preparing it for pickup.

Outlet

A term used to describe a single location of a fast-food chain.
It is often used interchangeably with "restaurant" or "store."

Outside Catering

A service offered by some fast-food chains where they
provide food and beverages for events outside of the
restaurant. This can include weddings, corporate events, and
other special occasions.

Owner-operator

A franchisee who is also the owner of the restaurant and is
directly involved in its day-to-day operations. This is in
contrast to franchisees who operate multiple locations and
delegate the day-to-day operations to managers.

Parent Company

The parent company of the fast food chain is the overarching entity that owns the brand and intellectual property rights associated with the chain. The parent company is responsible for providing support and resources to franchisees, as well as enforcing guidelines and standards to maintain brand consistency.

Payment Terms

Payment terms refer to the agreed-upon payment schedule between the franchisee and the parent company. These terms may include initial franchise fees, ongoing royalty payments, and marketing fees. Understanding and adhering to payment terms is crucial to maintaining a positive relationship with the parent company.

Performance Metrics

Performance metrics are measurements used to evaluate the success of a fast food chain franchisee. These metrics may include sales figures, customer satisfaction ratings, and employee turnover rates. Performance metrics are used to identify areas for improvement and opportunities for growth.

Personal Investment

Personal investment refers to the financial resources that a franchisee is willing to commit to the franchise opportunity. Personal investment may include the initial franchise fee, costs associated with securing a property lease, and ongoing operational expenses. The amount of personal investment required will vary depending on the fast food chain and the location of the franchise.

Pricing Strategy

Developing a pricing strategy is essential to the success of a fast food chain franchisee. The pricing strategy must consider factors such as competition, costs, and consumer demand. The parent company may provide pricing guidance and resources to help franchisees develop successful pricing strategies.

Product Line

The product line of a fast food chain refers to the menu items available for purchase. Establishing a diverse and innovative product line is crucial to attract and retain customers. The parent company may provide guidance and resources to help franchisees develop successful product lines.

Product Quality

Product quality is a crucial factor in the success of any fast food chain franchisee. Maintaining consistent, high-quality products is essential to retaining customers and building a positive reputation. The parent company may provide guidance and resources to ensure that all franchisees maintain high product quality standards.

Professional Development

Professional development refers to ongoing training and development opportunities available to franchisees. These opportunities are designed to improve skills and knowledge, increase efficiency, and maintain quality across all locations. The parent company may provide resources and support for ongoing professional development.

Profit Margin

The profit margin of a fast food chain is the difference between the revenue generated and the expenses incurred. Profit margins play a crucial role in the franchising process, as potential franchisees must weigh the potential costs against the potential profits. A higher profit margin means greater potential for success and profitability in the future.

Profitability Analysis

Profitability analysis is the process of evaluating the potential profitability of a fast food chain franchise. This analysis considers factors such as revenue, expenses, and competition to determine the potential for success. Conducting a profitability analysis is essential for franchisees to make informed decisions about the viability of the franchise opportunity.

Promotion

Promotion refers to marketing efforts aimed at increasing brand awareness and driving sales. As a franchisee, promoting the fast food chain is essential to attract and retain customers. The parent company may provide marketing support and resources to help franchisees develop effective promotional plans.

Property Lease

As a franchisee, securing a property lease is a crucial part of establishing a physical location for the fast food chain. Securing a favorable lease can result in significant cost savings and can impact the long-term success of the franchise.

Protocols

Protocols refer to established procedures and guidelines that must be followed by all franchisees. These protocols may include rules about inventory management, hiring policies, and customer service standards. Following established protocols is essential to maintain consistency and quality across all locations.

Public Image

Maintaining a positive public image is crucial for any fast food chain franchisee. Negative publicity or reviews can impact the reputation of the entire brand, leading to decreased sales and profitability. Franchisees must follow established protocols and maintain high standards of customer service to maintain a positive public image.

Purchasing Power

Purchasing power refers to the ability to buy goods and services at a lower cost due to the large quantity purchased. As part of a fast food chain, franchisees may have access to the parent company's purchasing power to buy ingredients and supplies at a lower cost. This can lead to cost savings for the franchisee and increased profitability.

Recurring Fees

Ongoing fees paid by franchisees, such as royalties, marketing and advertising fees, and other costs required to maintain the franchised location.

Regional Advertising

Advertising initiatives paid for by franchisees in a specific region, typically managed by the franchisor.

Regional Franchisee

A person or company who owns the rights to open and operate multiple franchised locations in a specific region or area.

Regional Meeting

A gathering of franchisees in a specific region to discuss business strategies, marketing, and other important aspects of running the franchise.

Renewal

The process of extending the term of a franchise agreement, usually for a set number of additional years.

Repairs and Maintenance

The responsibility of franchisees to maintain and repair their franchised location to ensure that it meets the brand standards and is safe for customers.

Required Investment

The minimum amount of capital required to open a franchised location, which includes a franchise fee, initial investment, and other expenses.

Required Training

The mandatory training that franchisees must complete before opening their location, including operational procedures, marketing strategies, and other important aspects of running the business.

Resale Value

The estimated value of a franchised location if the owner decides to sell it at a later time. This value can be affected by various factors such as location, profitability, and brand recognition.

Residual Income

Income generated by a franchised location after all expenses have been paid, often used as a gauge of profitability.

Restricted Products

Products that cannot be sold within a franchised location due to brand restrictions or legal limitations.

Return on Investment

The amount of profit generated by a franchised location, expressed as a percentage of the initial investment.

Right of First Refusal

A contractual clause that grants the franchisor the option to purchase a franchisee's location before it is sold to a third party.

Rights to Territory

The exclusive rights granted to a franchisee to operate within a specific geographic area, typically outlined in the franchise agreement.

Royalties

Fees paid by a franchisee to the franchisor for the use of their name and operating system, usually based on a percentage of gross revenue. Royalties also cover ongoing support, training, and other services provided by the franchisor.

Sales Data Analysis

Franchisees must be able to analyze sales data in order to make informed decisions about inventory management, pricing, and marketing. This may involve tracking metrics such as sales by item, average ticket size, and customer demographics.

Sales Volume

Sales volume refers to the total amount of revenue generated by a franchise location within a given time period. This metric is closely monitored by both franchisors and franchisees, as it is a key indicator of business performance and profitability.

Service Model

The service model, or the way in which customers are served at a fast food restaurant, can vary widely depending on the franchise. Some franchises may focus on drive-thru service, while others may emphasize dine-in or delivery options. The service model can affect everything from staffing needs to store layout and design.

Site Selection

Site selection is a crucial aspect of franchising a fast food chain. It involves choosing the right location for the restaurant, taking into account factors such as traffic, demographics, accessibility, and competition. The franchisor typically provides guidance and assistance in this process, but it ultimately falls on the franchisee to make a well-informed decision.

Social Media Marketing

Social media marketing can be a powerful tool for fast food franchises looking to engage with customers and build brand awareness. Franchisees may be responsible for creating and managing social media accounts, as well as developing campaigns and promotions to attract and retain customers.

Special Promotions

Fast food franchises often use special promotions, such as limited-time offers or loyalty programs, to attract and retain customers. Franchisees may be responsible for implementing these promotions and tracking their effectiveness.

Staff Training

Fast food franchises rely heavily on their staff to deliver high-quality service and uphold brand standards. Franchisees are responsible for training and managing their employees, which may include initial onboarding as well as ongoing development and performance monitoring.

Standardized Operating Procedures

Standardized operating procedures (SOPs) are step-by-step instructions for carrying out specific tasks and processes within a franchise. SOPs help ensure consistency and quality across all locations, as well as facilitate employee training and efficiency.

Start-up Costs

Franchisees must typically pay a variety of start-up costs, including initial franchise fees, equipment and inventory expenses, and marketing and advertising expenses. These costs can vary widely depending on the franchise and the location, and must be carefully considered before entering a franchise agreement.

Store Design

Fast food franchises rely on their store design and layout to create an inviting atmosphere and enhance the customer experience. Franchisees must follow established design guidelines and work with approved vendors to ensure that their stores meet system standards.

Supplies and Inventory

Fast food franchises require a steady supply chain to keep their restaurants stocked with necessary ingredients, packaging materials, and other supplies. Franchisees must work with approved suppliers and manage their inventory effectively to avoid shortages or waste.

Supply Chain Management

Effective supply chain management is essential for ensuring that franchise locations are well-stocked with necessary supplies and ingredients. This may involve working with multiple suppliers, managing inventory levels, and forecasting demand.

Supply Chain Partnerships

Fast food franchises may partner with suppliers or manufacturers to develop new products or improve existing ones. These partnerships can help franchisees differentiate themselves from competitors and drive sales growth.

Support Services

Franchisees typically receive ongoing support and guidance from the franchisor, including assistance with marketing, operations, training, and other aspects of running a successful business. These support services can be critical for new franchisees or those facing challenges.

System Standards

System standards are the guidelines and procedures that franchisees must follow in order to maintain consistency and quality across all franchise locations. These standards may cover everything from food preparation and service to employee uniforms and store design. Adherence to system standards is essential for building and maintaining a strong brand and reputation.

Technology Platform

A system or software program used by the franchisor to manage and support its franchise network, including functions such as inventory management, point-of-sale transactions, ordering, and reporting. The technology platform is a critical component of the franchising model, providing franchisees with access to real-time data and support.

Term

The length of time specified in the franchise agreement during which the franchisee has the exclusive right to operate a fast food chain outlet under the franchisor's name and using its business system. The term is usually renewable, subject to certain conditions, and is a critical factor in determining the long-term success of the franchisee's business.

Territory

A designated geographic area within which the franchisee
has exclusive rights to operate a fast food chain outlet. The
size and scope of the territory are usually defined by the
franchisor, depending on factors such as population density,
demand, and market potential.

Territory Development Agreement

A legal agreement between the franchisor and a franchisee
that outlines the terms and conditions for the franchisee to
open and operate multiple fast food chain outlets within a
specific geographic area over a specific period of time. The
territory development agreement is a valuable tool for both
the franchisor and the franchisee, as it allows for controlled
and strategic expansion of the franchise system.

Territory Fee

A fee charged by the franchisor to reserve a specific
geographic area for the exclusive use of a franchisee. The
territory fee is typically a one-time charge that is assessed at
the beginning of the franchise relationship, and is intended
to provide the franchisee with a protected market area in
which to operate its business.

Test Marketing

A limited-time marketing campaign designed to evaluate consumer demand and market potential for a new fast food chain product or service. Test marketing is often used by franchisors to refine their business models and ensure that new products are successful before being introduced to a wider market.

Total Investment

The total amount of capital required by the franchisee to set up and operate a fast food chain outlet, including costs such as franchise fees, equipment, inventory, and working capital. The total investment is a key element in the franchising agreement, as it determines the financial resources needed to launch the business.

Trademark

A symbol, logo, or other identifying mark or name that is registered and legally protected by the franchisor as a means of distinguishing its fast food chain from other competitors in the marketplace. The trademark is a valuable asset that helps to establish brand recognition and loyalty among customers.

Training Fees

Fees paid by the franchisee to cover the costs associated with attending the franchisor's training program. Training fees may include expenses such as travel, lodging, and materials, and are typically paid in advance of attending the training program.

Training Manual

A comprehensive instructional guide created by the franchisor and provided to franchisees to supplement the training program. The training manual provides detailed information and guidelines on all aspects of operating a fast food chain outlet, including policies, procedures, and best practices.

Training Platform

A digital or online system used by the franchisor to support and supplement its training program. The training platform may include features such as video tutorials, interactive simulations, and knowledge assessments, and is designed to enhance the learning experience for franchisees.

Training Program

A comprehensive and formal educational process offered by the franchisor to equip franchisees with the skills and knowledge required to manage and operate a fast food chain outlet. The training program typically covers areas such as food preparation, personnel management, franchise operations, and customer service.

Transfer Agreement

A legal agreement that outlines the terms and conditions under which a franchisee can sell or transfer ownership of a fast food chain outlet to a new owner. The transfer agreement is an important document that protects the interests of both the franchisor and the franchisee, and ensures a smooth transition for the business.

Transfer Fee

A fee charged by the franchisor when a franchisee sells or transfers ownership of a fast food chain outlet to a new owner. The transfer fee is designed to cover the administrative costs associated with transferring the franchise agreement, and may vary depending on the terms of the original franchise agreement.

Transnational Franchising

A form of franchising in which the franchisor enters into agreements with franchisees in different countries around the world. Transnational franchising is a complex and detailed process that requires careful consideration of international laws, regulations, and cultural differences.

Validation

Validation is the process of verifying and assessing the performance of a franchisee's outlet against pre-defined standards and criteria set by the franchisor. This can include regular inspections, quality control assessments, and mystery-shopping exercises, as well as the collection of sales and operational data. Validation is an essential tool for franchisors to enforce brand standards, maintain control over customer experience, and ensure that franchisees are delivering on the promises made to consumers.

Validation Schedule

A validation schedule is the timeline and frequency with which fast food franchisors conduct validation activities for franchisees. The schedule may include regular inspections, audits, mystery shops, or other assessments, and is usually designed to ensure compliance with brand standards, assess performance, and identify areas for improvement. The validation schedule is an important tool for ensuring consistency and quality across the franchise system.

Value Engineering

Value engineering is a systematic approach to reducing costs while improving quality and performance. In the fast food industry, value engineering may involve re-evaluating recipes, menu items, or processes to identify areas where materials or labor can be reduced without sacrificing quality or customer experience. Effective value engineering can help franchisees streamline operations, reduce waste, and improve profitability.

Value Menu

A value menu is a menu offering a variety of items at a low price point, typically below $1.00 per item. Value menus are often used as a promotional tool to drive traffic and increase sales volume, and can be an effective way for fast food franchises to compete on price with other brands.

Value Proposition

A franchise's value proposition is the unique combination of product, service, pricing, and marketing that sets it apart from its competitors and makes it attractive to customers. In the fast food industry, value propositions can range from offering high-quality food at a low price point to providing speedy service and convenience to customers on-the-go. Franchisees must understand and effectively communicate their value proposition to consumers in order to attract and retain customers.

Variance

Variance refers to the difference between actual performance and expected performance for a given metric or KPI. In the fast food industry, variances may be calculated for metrics such as sales volume, customer traffic, or food costs. High variances can indicate inefficiencies, inconsistencies, or problems within a franchise system that may require corrective action.

Vendor Agreements

Vendor agreements are contractual agreements between fast food franchisors and vendors specifying terms and conditions for the purchase of goods and services, including pricing, delivery, quality control, and termination. Vendor agreements are crucial for maintaining supply chain consistency and quality, protecting the brand reputation, and ensuring compliance with legal and regulatory requirements. Franchisees must carefully review and negotiate vendor agreements to ensure that their rights and interests are protected.

Vendor Management

Vendor management is the process of selecting, negotiating with, and managing vendors for a fast food franchise system. This can include sourcing new vendors, negotiating contracts, monitoring performance and quality, and resolving issues or disputes that arise. Effective vendor management is critical to ensuring high quality, consistent supplies at a reasonable cost.

Vendor Rebates

Vendor rebates refer to cash or other incentives provided by vendors to fast food franchisors based on volume or other purchasing criteria. These rebates can be significant sources of income for franchisors, and can help to offset the costs of supporting franchisees in areas such as marketing, training, and technology. Franchisees may also benefit indirectly from vendor rebates through lower supply costs.

Vendor Relationships

Vendor relationships are the partnerships and collaborations between fast food franchisors and their approved vendors. These relationships can be critical to the success of the franchise system, as they can provide access to high-quality supplies and equipment, favorable pricing and terms, and ongoing support and training. Strong vendor relationships are built on trust, transparency, and shared goals and values.

Vendor Support

Vendor support refers to the support offered by a fast food franchisor to its franchisees in sourcing, selecting, and purchasing supplies, equipment, and merchandise from approved vendors. The franchisor typically negotiates favorable prices and terms at the national or regional level with suppliers, which the franchisee is then able to pass on to individual store level. Effective vendor support can help franchisees reduce costs and improve profitability, while ensuring consistency and quality across locations.

Viable Location

A viable location is a site for a fast food franchise that is expected to generate sufficient demand and profitability to justify the investment required to operate the business. Factors that may contribute to a viable location include foot traffic, nearby businesses and institutions, population density, and accessibility by car or public transportation. Franchisees must carefully evaluate potential locations before making a commitment to ensure the long-term viability of the business.

Vision

A franchise system's vision is its long-term plan for growth, development, and success. A strong vision can inspire franchisees and align the brand around a common purpose, while also providing a roadmap for decision-making and strategic planning. A franchise system's vision may encompass goals such as expanding into new markets, developing innovative products or services, improving customer experience, or promoting social responsibility.

Vital Signs

Vital signs are a set of key performance indicators (KPIs) used by fast food franchises to monitor the health and performance of their franchise system. These indicators typically include metrics such as unit growth, same-store sales growth, profitability, customer satisfaction, and employee turnover. By tracking these vital signs, franchisors can quickly identify areas of weakness within the system, diagnose problems, and implement corrective actions to ensure the long-term success of the brand.

Volume Discounts

Volume discounts are discounts offered by vendors to fast food franchisees based on the quantity of products or services purchased. These discounts can be an attractive incentive for franchisees to purchase from preferred suppliers, and can help to keep supply costs low. However, volume discounts must be carefully balanced against quality control and consistency, as franchisees should not sacrifice quality for cost savings.

Wages

The compensation paid to employees for their work. In a franchise, it is important to have clear guidelines on how employee wages are determined and how they fit within the overall operating costs. This can include factors such as minimum wage laws, industry standards, and individual franchisee policies.

Warranty

A guarantee provided by the franchisor or supplier that the equipment or products used in the fast food chain are free from defects and will function as intended. It is important for franchisees to understand the terms of any warranties provided in order to ensure they are in compliance with contractual obligations.

Waste Reduction

Efforts to minimize the amount of waste generated by the fast food chain, including food waste, packaging waste, and energy waste. As a franchisee, it is important to implement effective waste reduction strategies in order to reduce operating costs and minimize the chain's environmental impact.

Water Conservation

Efforts to minimize the amount of water used by the fast food chain, including installing water-efficient fixtures and equipment, training employees to conserve water, and implementing landscaping practices that require minimal irrigation. Conserving water is an important part of sustainable business practices.

Wayfinding

The process of designing and mapping a customer's journey through the fast food chain. Effective wayfinding can help increase sales by encouraging customers to navigate the restaurant and find what they are looking for without becoming overwhelmed or frustrated.

Website

The online presence of the fast food chain. A website can provide valuable information to potential customers, including menus, locations, hours of operation, and special promotions. As a franchisee, it is important to maintain a strong website and online presence in order to attract and retain customers.

Wellness Program

A program offered to employees of the fast food chain designed to promote health and wellness. Wellness programs can include things like fitness classes, health screenings, and nutrition education. As a franchisee, implementing a wellness program can help improve employee morale and productivity.

Wholesale

The purchasing of large quantities of food or supplies from suppliers for use in the fast food chain. As a franchisee, it is important to have strong relationships with high-quality suppliers in order to obtain the best prices and ensure a consistent supply of goods.

WiFi

A wireless internet connection that is available to customers at the fast food chain. Offering free WiFi can be a valuable marketing tool, as it encourages customers to stay longer and can help generate repeat business.

Withholding

The process of deducting income tax, social security, and other payments from employee wages on behalf of the government. As a franchisee, it is important to understand and comply with all applicable withholding requirements to avoid legal and financial penalties.

Work-life Balance

The balance between a franchisee's work obligations and their personal life. Work-life balance is important for maintaining good health and avoiding burnout. As a franchisee, it is important to prioritize self-care and maintain a healthy work-life balance.

Workers' Compensation

Insurance that provides benefits to employees who are injured or become ill as a result of their work. As a franchisee, it is important to obtain workers' compensation insurance to protect both employees and the business in the event of a workplace injury.

Workforce

The group of people who work for the fast food chain. As a franchisee, it is important to select and manage a strong workforce in order to maintain the brand's standards and reputation. This includes recruiting, training, and retaining employees who are committed to providing quality service to customers.

Workforce Management Software

Software designed to assist with managing employee schedules, payroll, and other workforce related tasks. Workforce management software can help automate and streamline many of the administrative tasks associated with managing a fast food chain.

Workplace Safety

The process of identifying and mitigating potential hazards in the fast food chain, including physical hazards, chemical hazards, and ergonomic hazards. Workplace safety is important for protecting employees and avoiding legal and financial liabilities.